Classical Literature

Comprehension Activities to Develop Interest in Reading

Grades 3–4

Written by

George Moore

Published by World Teachers Press®

Published with the permission of R.I.C. Publications Pty. Ltd.

First published by R.I.C. Publications Pty. Ltd., Perth, Western Australia. Revised by Didax Educational Resources.

Distributed in Canada by Scholar's Choice.

Printed in the United States of America.

Order Number 2-5173
ISBN 1-58324-100-0

A B C D E F 03 02 01 00

Educational Resources
395 Main Street
Rowley, MA 01969
www.worldteacherspress.com

Foreword

The story summaries featured in this book are derived from classic tales which have delighted children and adults for generations. Even if the children in today's schools have not read the original stories, they have met some of fiction's greatest characters through feature films, full-length cartoons and television series based on these classic books. Filmmakers from different eras are constantly returning to these classics because their storylines are so interesting, so it is hoped children in schools today will also be familiar with our rich literary heritage and will, at some time in their lives, read these great books and those from other countries around the world.

Table of Contents

Teachers Notes

 lot of reading provided for students reflects modern society and the interests and views of contemporary educators and students alike. It is becoming more recognized that this form of reading, while being appropriate to modern-day society, does not provide any history of reading, writers, or of authors themselves. Many authors of the past wrote material that can best be described as "Classic." This book aims to bring students a taste of the "Classics" so that their interest and imagination can be sparked to encourage them to read more Classical Literature.

By investigating classical literature it can be argued:

(a) That literature can be based on actuality or fantasy and includes written and oral texts, films, plays, poems, novels, legends, biographies, etc.

(b) That students should study literature from other countries which has been translated into English.

(c) That through reading and critically responding to literature, students extend their understanding of the world and themselves.

(d) That a wide range of literature should be available and should include shared experiences such as those experienced when a class enjoys a video or a teacher's reading as a group.

(e) That examination of the different values of other times is important in the study of literature stories/topics.

(f) Classic literature refers to works recognized over time as excellent examples of their type.

The summaries of the stories are open-ended in order to encourage students to read the suggested junior fiction books and discover for themselves what happens.

The stories are sequenced in an approximate order of difficulty and teachers notes are provided.

The "R" at the bottom of every third page denotes additional reading and literature appreciation activities.

 # Teachers Notes

❖ Sentence

A sentence must contain a verb which has a subject and make complete sense. These examples are not sentences as they do not make complete sense.

    (a) went down the road   (b) John saw a   (c) Lucie laughed at

❖ Periods

Periods are used to end a sentence and for most abbreviations (Mr., Mrs., Dr., etc., e.g.). As a rule, we do not use periods after the letter representing well-known organizations such as a government agency, network call letters, acronyms or radio/TV stations (FBI, IBM, NBC, MADD, POW) or initials of a prominent person (JFK).

❖ Capital Letters

Capital letters are used for proper nouns which are the names of people or places, for the first words of sentences and for special words like months, days of the week, etc.

❖ Antonyms (opposites)

Opposites are words that are opposite in meaning, for example, hot and cold, tall and short.

❖ Adjectives

Adjectives are words which describe nouns or words which stand for nouns (pronouns). Adjectives are usually seen in front of a noun or after a linking verb as in "the man is *rich*."

❖ Key Words

Key words are important words surrounded by other words and phrases which add information to the key words.

❖ Rhyming Words

Rhyming words are words which have the same sound but usually the initial consonants are different (e.g., mine, line), the initial digraphs differ (e.g., chess, bless) or one word has no initial consonant (e.g., age, page).

Jakob and Wilhelm Grimm collected fairy tales from all over the world but especially those from Germany. Jakob became a private librarian to a European king and was able to read rare books about ancient folk tales. The brothers advised their assistants to listen to old stories told by poor peasants and then retold them in print.

Rumplestiltskin

A miller tells the king that his beautiful daughter can spin gold from straw. This greedy king locks her in his palace so she can make him rich. The poor girl can't spin straw into gold but a strange little man helps her. Because he helps her, she gives him gifts. Soon she has no more gifts to give him. He then tells her she can give him her first baby after she marries the king.

Later, the odd little man feels sorry for her. He says that if she can guess his name she can keep her child. This tale does have a happy ending. I wonder how she finds out what he is called?

Read one of these junior fiction books:

Fairies and Fables – R. Mathias Hamlyn

The Story of Rumplestiltskin – a version by J. Langley

The Fairy Tale Treasury – V. Haviland

Rumplestiltskin

1. What did the miller tell the king?

_____

_____

2. Where did the king live?

_____

3. Color yes or no.

   (a)   The miller told the truth.

yes	no

   (b)   The king was greedy.

yes	no

   (c)   The girl was pretty.

yes	no

   (d)   The miller's daughter married the king.

yes	no

   (e)   The new queen guesses the little man's name.

yes	no

4. What do you think the strange little man is called?

_____

5. Find a word in the story that means the same.

   (a) wealthy _____   (b) small _____

   (c) presents _____   (d) story _____

   (e) odd _____

6. List four things that could be made from gold.

_____

_____

_____

_____

7. What gold things would you like to spin from straw?

_____

_____

_____

_____

Rumplestiltskin

1. The jumbled words below are all clothes.
   Unjumble each word to find out how to color the picture.

   (a) aht _____ (red)

   (b) tsrih _____ (green)

   (c) obost _____ (brown)

   (d) tsnpa _____ (orange)

   (e) elbt _____ (black)

2. Find words from the story to rhyme with these.

   (a) dress _____

   (b) chin _____

   (c) rocks _____

   (d) saw _____

3. (a) What kind of job do you think the "miller" in the story would do?

   _____

   (b) A miller is a very old job. Can you explain what each person would do in these jobs from olden times?

   (i) carpenter _____

   (ii) tailor _____

   (iii) huntsman _____

   (iv) blacksmith _____

   (v) cobbler _____

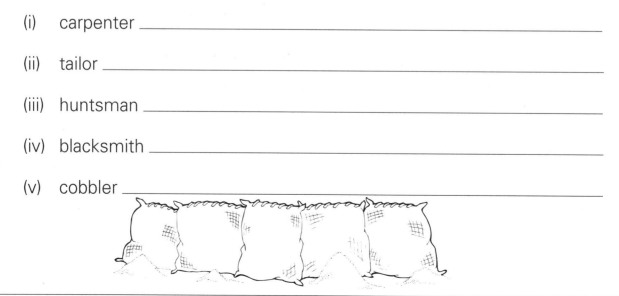

The Tale of Peter Rabbit was first published about 100 years ago. Beatrix Potter's rich parents had her educated at home with a governess so she was a lonely child, as her brother went to school. She started to write and illustrate her own books for young friends and a sick child she knew. Potter died in 1943 and her home in England is now open to the public.

The Tale of Peter Rabbit

Four young rabbits called Flopsy, Mopsy, Cottontail and Peter live with their mother. Their home is in a burrow under the roots of a huge fir tree. The little rabbits are warned about going into Mr. McGregor's garden. This is because their father had been caught there and put in a pie by Mrs. McGregor. Peter doesn't listen to his mother and eats vegetables in the garden. He is seen by the owner so he hides in the tool shed.

After escaping from the shed, he can't find a way out of the garden. He avoids a white cat, but even a mouse can't help him to get out. I wonder if Peter is made into rabbit pie as well?

Read this junior fiction book:

The Tale of Peter Rabbit – B. Potter

The Tale of Peter Rabbit

1. Name the four children in the Rabbit family.

_____

_____

_____

_____

2. Why didn't mother rabbit want her children to go into the garden?

_____

3. Color the correct word.

(a)   The Rabbit family lived in a | shed | tree | burrow | .

(b)   There are | three | four | five | members of the Rabbit family.

(c)   A | white | black | grey | cat chased Peter.

4. Check the correct answer.

(a)   Peter liked to eat: fruit. ☐   vegetables. ☐   meat. ☐

(b)   Peter hid from Mr. McGregor:

behind a fir tree. ☐   under a bush. ☐   in the tool shed. ☐

5. Find the opposite of these words in the story.

(a)   black _____

(b)   tiny _____

(c)   old _____

(d)   over _____

(e)   can _____

(f)   in _____

6. Read and draw.

Peter is hiding from Mr. McGregor in the tool shed.

The Tale of Peter Rabbit

1. A wild rabbit lives in a

_____.

Match each animal to its home.

(a) bear •   • stable

(b) pig •   • shell

(c) bee •   • web

(d) spider •   • hive

(e) horse •   • den

(f) snail •   • sty

2. Draw and label the home a pet rabbit would live in.

It is called a _____.

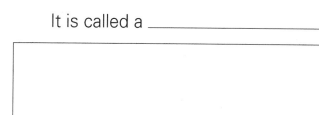

3. Color each vegetable correctly. Circle the ones you think Peter would like.

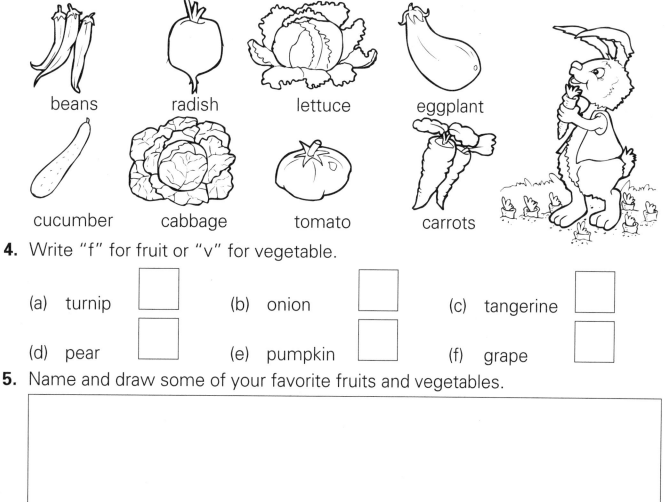

beans   radish   lettuce   eggplant

cucumber   cabbage   tomato   carrots

4. Write "f" for fruit or "v" for vegetable.

(a) turnip ☐   (b) onion ☐   (c) tangerine ☐

(d) pear ☐   (e) pumpkin ☐   (f) grape ☐

5. Name and draw some of your favorite fruits and vegetables.

Dr. Seuss was the pen name of an American writer, Theodor Geisel, who died in 1991. This book was published in 1957 and uses only 175 different words to tell a funny, rhyming story. Geisel wrote more than 40 books of nonsense verse and comic pictures he drew himself. He won an Academy Award for his animated cartoon "Gerald McBoing Boing."

The Cat in the Hat

On a cold, wet day, Sally and her brother are sitting in the house all alone. They are bored and have nothing to do. Soon, a strange cat wearing a funny hat comes in through the front door. He tells them they can have fun, even on a wet day when the sun isn't shining. The cat then juggles a cake, books, a goldfish in a bowl and many other things.

He also shows them Thing 1 and Thing 2, who run out from his large, red wooden box. These two odd little creatures fly kites inside the house. The goldfish doesn't like what is happening at all! It wants the children to get rid of the cat and his friends. I wonder what Sally's mother will say when she returns home?

Read this junior fiction book or view this video:

The Cat in the Hat – Dr. Seuss

The Cat in the Hat – video

The Cat in the Hat

1. Why were Sally and her brother bored?

   _____

   _____

2. Where do you think Sally's mother had gone?

   _____

3. Who taught the children to have fun even on a wet day?

   _____

4. Draw Thing 1 and Thing 2 and what they did in the house.

5. Color yes or no.

   (a) The cat was good at juggling. | yes | no |

   (b) The goldfish was happy. | yes | no |

   (c) Thing 1 and Thing 2 were in a green box. | yes | no |

   (d) Mother was at home. | yes | no |

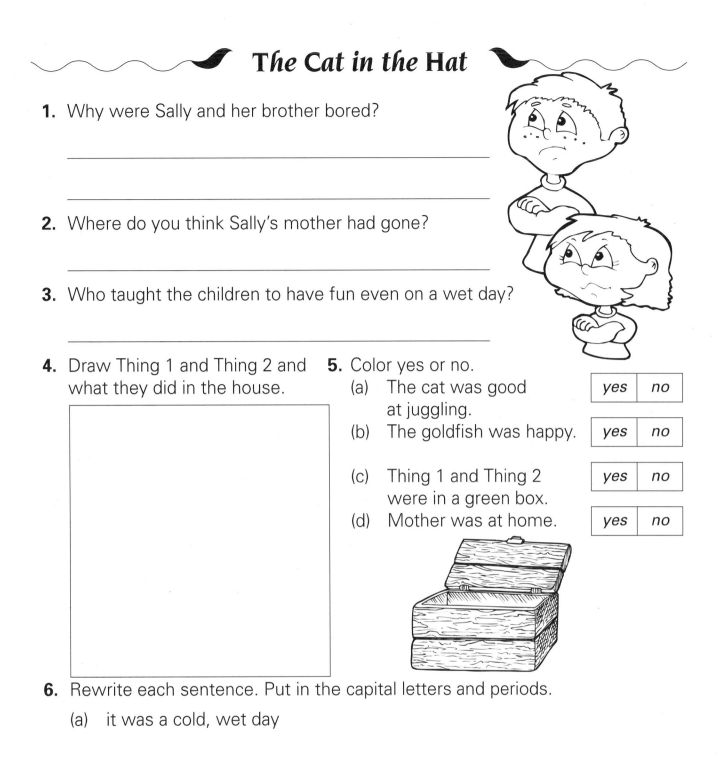

6. Rewrite each sentence. Put in the capital letters and periods.

   (a) it was a cold, wet day

   _____

   (b) the strange cat wore a funny hat

   _____

7. Do you think the children's mother will be happy when she returns home?

   _____ Why/Why not? _____

   _____

   _____

The Cat in the Hat

1. List some things you like to do on a cold, wet day. Draw a picture of you doing one of them.

   _____

   _____

   _____

   _____

2. The word "goldfish" is a compound word.
   It is made up of two words, gold + fish.
   Use the picture clues to find these compound words.

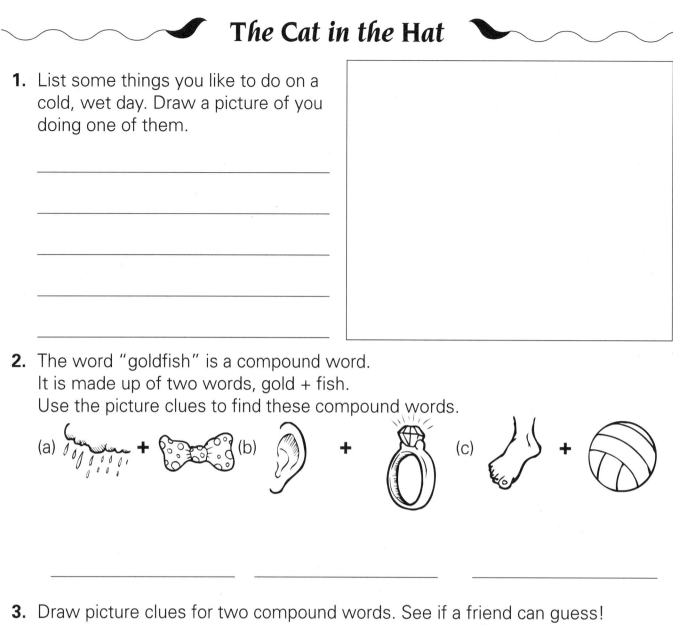

   (a) _____ _____ (c) _____

3. Draw picture clues for two compound words. See if a friend can guess!

4. Write these words in alphabetical order.

   cake   books   goldfish   bowl

   _____

   _____

The Hare and the Tortoise

A long time ago, a hare is boasting to his animal friends. He brags how fast he is and dares any animal to run against him. A tortoise is the only creature who will race him. The hare thinks this is a joke.

"Let's see what happens," says the tortoise.

The hare dashes off. He is so confident of winning he stops to have a little nap on the grass. The tortoise doesn't stop for a rest at all. He just keeps plodding along very, very slowly. By the time the hare wakes up, will the tortoise have won the race? What do you think?

Read one of these junior fiction books:

Aesop's Fables (Illustrated Stories for Children) – a version with illustrations by C. Santore

Aesop's Fables – a version with illustrations by L. Zwerger

Aesop's Fables – a version by R. Piumini

Nursery Tales Around the World – edited by J. Sierra

The Hare and the Tortoise

1. Why did the hare want to be in a race? _____

    _____

2. Which animal decided to race the hare? _____

3. Why do you think the hare thought it was a joke to race this animal?

    _____

    _____

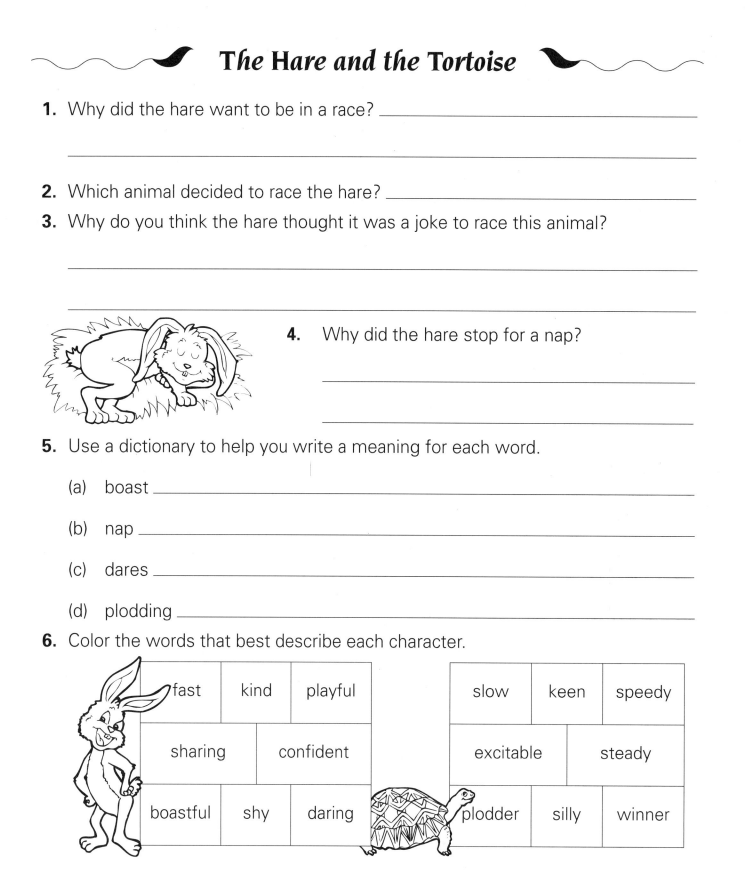

4. Why did the hare stop for a nap?

    _____

    _____

5. Use a dictionary to help you write a meaning for each word.

    (a) boast _____

    (b) nap _____

    (c) dares _____

    (d) plodding _____

6. Color the words that best describe each character.

fast	kind	playful
sharing	confident	
boastful	shy	daring

slow	keen	speedy
excitable		steady
plodder	silly	winner

7. Would you rather be like the hare or the tortoise? _____

    Give a reason for your answer. _____

    _____

Classical Literature   World Teachers Press®

The Hare and the Tortoise

1. Use the pictures to help you find out the differences between a tortoise and a sea turtle.

Put a ✔ or a ✗ in the grid.

	reptile	dome-shaped shell	streamlined shell	lives on land	lives in water	has feet	has flippers
tortoise							
sea turtle							

2. Now use the pictures to help you find out the differences between a hare and a rabbit.

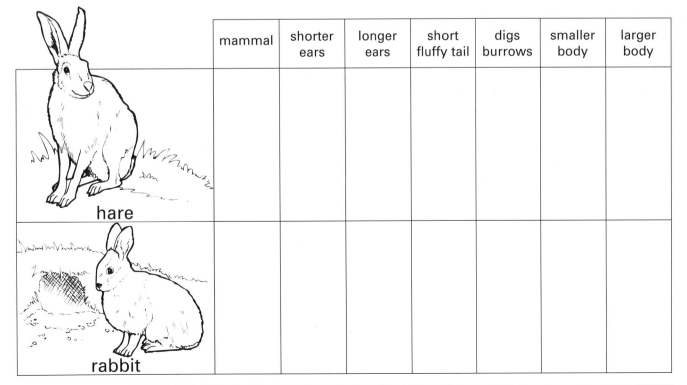

	mammal	shorter ears	longer ears	short fluffy tail	digs burrows	smaller body	larger body
hare							
rabbit							

This story was well known in France and other countries hundreds of years ago. A French poet, Charles Perrault, first published the story in the 17th Century. It was one of the first folk tales to be translated into English in 1729. In many fairy tales, the characters are described simply as "ugly," "bad" or "beautiful," just like Cinderella and her sisters. Several operas and ballets have been written around this tale and it is a popular English pantomime story. The story appears in the collected tales by the Grimm Brothers.

Cinderella

Cinderella has a cruel stepmother who has two vain, bossy daughters. The kind, gentle Cinderella is made to do all the housework in her ragged clothes. One day, her stepsisters are invited to a splendid ball for the king's son. A tearful Cinderella longs to go but is told she can't. Then her fairy godmother appears. She sends Cinderella to the dance in a golden coach. But she must leave at midnight before the coach changes back into a pumpkin.

The prince and Cinderella dance together all night and he invites her to another ball. When the clock strikes twelve, she flees from the ballroom and the prince is very sad. In her hurry to leave, Cinderella leaves behind her glass slipper. The prince's loyal servants then search the land to find the owner of the shoe. Will they discover that it belongs to the beautiful Cinderella?

Read one of these junior fiction books:

The Fairy Tale Treasury – V. Haviland
The Candlewick Book of Fairy Tales – S. Hayes

Cinderella

1. Explain how Cinderella got to go to the ball.

_____

_____

_____

_____

2. How can we tell the prince likes Cinderella?

_____

_____

3. Number these events from the story in the correct order.

(a)   The prince dances with Cinderella.

(b)   Cinderella's stepsisters are invited to the ball.

(c)   Cinderella drops her glass slipper.

(d)   Cinderella's fairy godmother appears.

(e)   Cinderella arrives at the ball.

(f)   Cinderella does all the work for her cruel stepmother.

4. Find a word from the story that means the opposite.

(a)   midday   _____

(b)   sons   _____

(c)   ugly   _____

(d)   arrives   _____

(e)   happy   _____

(f)   disappears   _____

5. Draw hands on the clock to show the time Cinderella had to leave the ball.

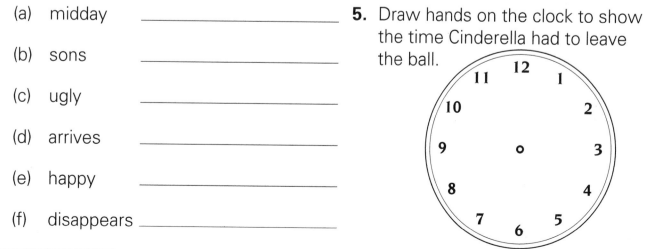

Cinderella

1. Choose a character from the story to finish the report.

Name _____

Lives with _____

_____

at _____.

Is | kind | mean, | beautiful | ugly,

| rich | poor, | happy | sad.

Likes to _____

_____

2. There are different types of shoes. For example, Cinderella wore a glass slipper. Fill in the missing letters to find the shoe names below.

(a) b____o____

(b) sa____ ____ ____l

(c) t____ ____ ____g

(d) cl____ ____

(e) sn____ ____k____ ____

(f) mo____ ____asi____

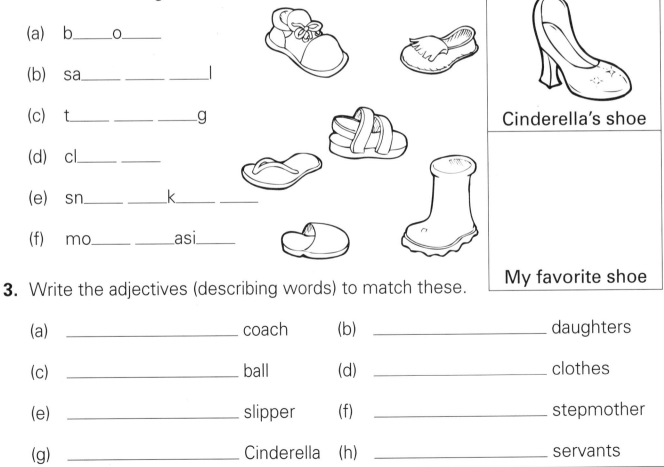

Cinderella's shoe

My favorite shoe

3. Write the adjectives (describing words) to match these.

(a) _____ coach

(b) _____ daughters

(c) _____ ball

(d) _____ clothes

(e) _____ slipper

(f) _____ stepmother

(g) _____ Cinderella

(h) _____ servants

Classical Literature World Teachers Press®

The German composer, Engelbert Humperdinck, wrote an opera about Hansel and Gretel which was first seen in 1893. Stories like this are also found in the folk tales of India and Japan. Hansel and Gretel were like many peasant children of these early times who were sent out to look after themselves because their poor parents could not support them.

Hansel and Gretel

Hansel and his young sister, Gretel, live near a forest. They live with their woodcutter father and stepmother, who are very poor. The wicked stepmother doesn't like children and plans to lose them deep in the forest. Hansel knows about her evil plan and drops small pebbles on the ground so they can find their way back home again. Once more their parents leave them in the forest. This time Hansel drops breadcrumbs because he can't get pebbles. Birds eat the crumbs and the children are lost!

By this time, the children are very hungry. Soon they find a strange house made of gingerbread, cake and candy. They both enjoy a meal. The cottage belongs to a witch who eats children attracted to her house. Will Hansel and Gretel find their way home this time?

Read one of these junior fiction books:

Hansel and Gretel – a version by J. Marshall

Hansel and Gretel – a version by R. Lesser

Hansel and Gretel – a version by E. Quarrie

Hansel and Gretel – a version by A. Bell

Hansel and Gretel

1. Why did Hansel and Gretel's parents take them to the deep forest?

_____

_____

2. Hansel and Gretel tried to return home twice. Write key words to explain how they tried.

… using pebbles	… using bread crumbs

3. Describe the unusual house the children found. Draw it.

_____

_____

_____

4. Who lived there?

_____

5. True or False.

(a) The father was a woodcutter. | true | false |

(b) The stepmother was kind. | true | false |

(c) The children couldn't find the pebble path to follow home. | true | false |

(d) Hansel knew about his stepmother's plans. | true | false |

(e) The children ate some of the witch's house. | true | false |

6. How do you think the story ends? Write your answer on the back of this page.

Hansel and Gretel

1. The word "stepmother" is a compound word.
It is made up of two words, step + mother.
Use the picture clues to find these compound words.

(a) [pan] + [cake] (b) [egg] + [plant] (c) [basket] + [ball]

_____ _____ _____

2. Find and write two more compound words from the story.

_____ _____

3. Find words from the story to finish these phrases.

(a) _____ stepmother

(b) hungry _____

(c) _____ house

(d) _____ pebbles

(e) _____ plan

4. Find words from the story that rhyme

(a) mouse _____

(b) steep _____

(c) ditch _____

(d) make _____

(e) track _____

5. Write sentences to describe this part of the story.

_____

_____

_____

_____

_____

_____

_____

Joseph Jacobs first introduced children to the story of "Jack and the Beanstalk" in his book "English Fairy Tales" written in 1890. Jacobs was born in Sydney, Australia, and emigrated to England in 1872. He was the first writer to prepare folk tales specifically for children. Jacobs left out any brutal parts and adapted the language for young readers. Similar stories about Jack, a giant killer, are found in other countries, such as France and Russia.

Jack and the Beanstalk

Jack is an only son who lives with his mother. They are very poor. As they have no money, Jack takes the family cow to sell at the local market. On the way, an old man gets Jack to swap the cow for some magic beans. Jack's mother is very angry and throws the beans out of the window. The next morning they find that a beanstalk has grown up to the sky like a big ladder.

Jack climbs the stalk and finds the castle of a rich giant. When the huge ogre comes home, his wife feels sorry for Jack. She knows her husband likes eating little boys on toast, so she hides Jack in the oven. I wonder what happens to him and a hen that lays golden eggs?

Read one of these junior fiction books:

The Fairy Tale Treasury – V. Haviland

Jack and The Beanstalk – a version by P. Galdone

Jack and The Beanstalk – a version by S. Kellogg

Jack and the Beanstalk

1. Fill in the missing words.

_____ is an _____

son who lives with his _____ .

They are very _____ .

He takes a _____ to sell at the

_____ but swaps the cow for

some _____ _____ .

2. Why was Jack's mother angry?

_____

_____

3. Where does the beanstalk lead to? _____

4. List three facts about the giant inside this shape.

5. What other word is used for giant in this story?

_____

6. Why did the giant's wife hide Jack?

_____

_____

7. Jack was hidden in the

 □ bin.   □ oven.   □ cupboard.

8. What would you do with a hen that lays golden eggs?

_____

_____

Jack and the Beanstalk

1. Use the clues to find the mystery word. _____

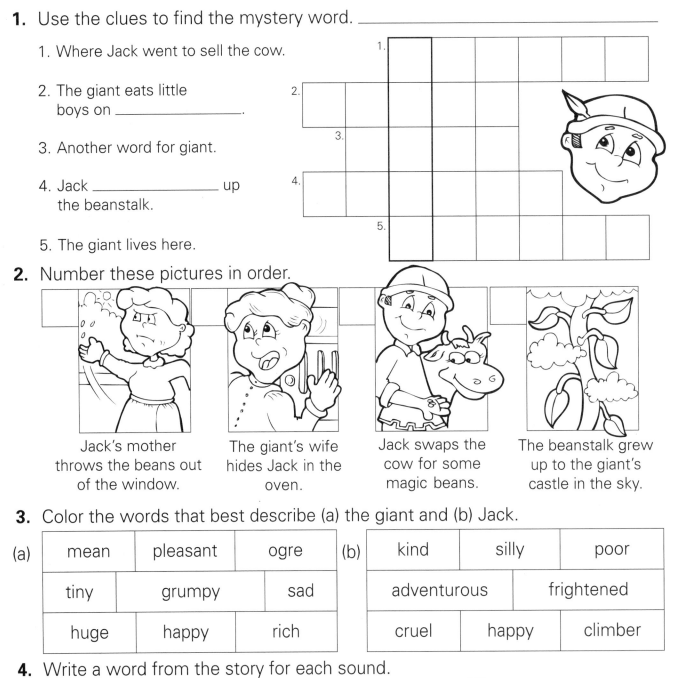

   1. Where Jack went to sell the cow.

   2. The giant eats little boys on _____.

   3. Another word for giant.

   4. Jack _____ up the beanstalk.

   5. The giant lives here.

2. Number these pictures in order.

| Jack's mother throws the beans out of the window. | The giant's wife hides Jack in the oven. | Jack swaps the cow for some magic beans. | The beanstalk grew up to the giant's castle in the sky. |

3. Color the words that best describe (a) the giant and (b) Jack.

(a)

mean	pleasant	ogre
tiny	grumpy	sad
huge	happy	rich

(b)

kind	silly	poor
adventurous		frightened
cruel	happy	climber

4. Write a word from the story for each sound.

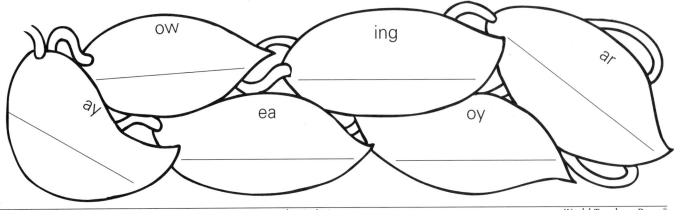

ow   ing   ar

ay   ea   oy

In some hot, dry parts of Australia there are frogs which survive droughts by filling themselves with water. When they are swollen they bury themselves under the soil until the rains come again. During droughts, Aboriginal Australians used to dig them up for the water they contained. It is believed these frogs could be descendants of Tiddalik, an animal from the Dreaming when Aboriginal Australians' Ancestors created the Earth.

Tiddalik

Tiddalik is a giant frog in stories from Australia. He lived a very long time ago in the Dreaming. One hot summer morning he is very thirsty. He drinks all the water in creeks, lakes and billabongs. Then he settles down to rest, for he can't move around with so much water inside him.

With no water, the trees begin to die and the animals and birds are unhappy. They decide to make Tiddalik laugh. Then the water inside him will pour out. The emus dance. Some animals play leapfrog. A noisy kookaburra laughs at his own funny stories, but Tiddalik doesn't even smile. I wonder which animal finally makes him laugh?

Read this junior fiction book:

From the Dreamtime – J. Ellis

Tiddalik

1. Why did Tiddalik drink so much water?

_____

_____

2. Do you think it was fair of Tiddalik to drink all of the water? Explain your answer.

_____

_____

3. List three things the animals tried to make Tiddalik laugh.

(a) _____

(b) _____

(c) _____

4. Explain how you would make Tiddalik laugh.

_____

_____

5. (a) What is a billabong?

_____

_____

_____

(b) Draw one of the animals in the story in the billabong.

6. What do you think will happen when Tiddalik does laugh?

_____

_____

Tiddalik

1. Find the opposite of these words in the story.

   (a) cry _____

   (b) happy _____

   (c) outside _____

   (d) cold _____

   (e) up _____

   (f) quiet _____

2. Read and draw.
   Tiddalik before and after drinking all the water.

   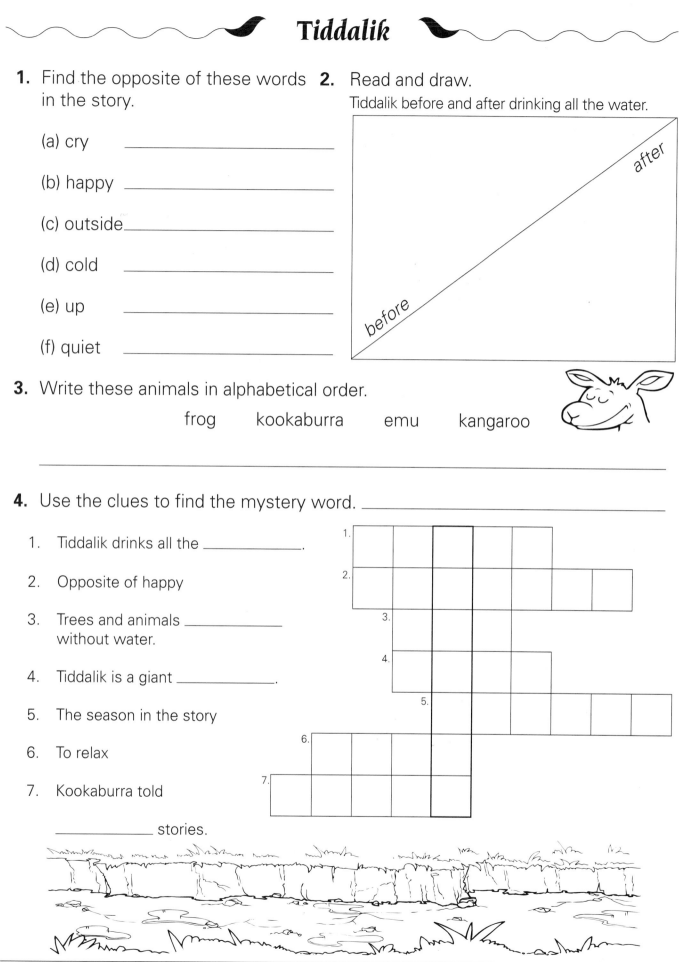

   after

   before

3. Write these animals in alphabetical order.

   frog   kookaburra   emu   kangaroo

_____

4. Use the clues to find the mystery word. _____

   1. Tiddalik drinks all the _____.

   2. Opposite of happy

   3. Trees and animals _____ without water.

   4. Tiddalik is a giant _____.

   5. The season in the story

   6. To relax

   7. Kookaburra told

   _____ stories.

The Grimm Brothers, Jakob and Wilhelm, both studied law at a university. Their first volume of collected fairy stories was published in 1812. The character of Snow White also appears in their story "Snow White and Rose Red." Walt Disney's company made the first full-length animated film of this story in 1937.

Snow White

Snow White grows up with her father and wicked stepmother, who is also the queen. The queen is jealous of the young girl's beauty. She orders a huntsman to kill Snow White in the forest. But he feels sorry for her and sets her free. She then lives with seven kind dwarfs in their small cottage in the forest. Soon, the queen finds out and tries to get rid of Snow White with a poisoned comb. The dwarfs save Snow White who is very ill.

Later the mean queen tries again with a poisoned apple. Thinking Snow White is dead, the dwarfs leave her on a mountain top in a glass coffin. They cry as they watch over her. Then a prince passes by and falls in love with Snow White. The dwarfs take pity on the young prince and say he can take her back to his father's palace. The prince's servants begin to move the coffin. As they do, a piece of poisoned apple falls out of Snow White's mouth. She wakes and is alive again. Later she marries the prince. But I wonder what happens to the wicked queen?

Read this junior fiction book:

Snow White: A Tale from the Brothers Grimm – a version with illustrations by C. Santore

Snow White

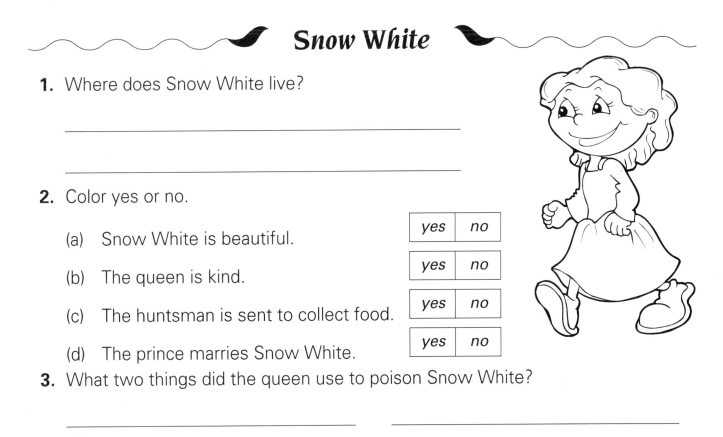

1. Where does Snow White live?

_____

_____

2. Color yes or no.

(a)   Snow White is beautiful.

| yes | no |

(b)   The queen is kind.

| yes | no |

(c)   The huntsman is sent to collect food.

| yes | no |

(d)   The prince marries Snow White.

| yes | no |

3. What two things did the queen use to poison Snow White?

_____   _____

4. Write numbers to show the correct order of these events in the story.

(a)   The sad dwarfs watch over the glass coffin.

| |

(b)   The queen tries to kill Snow White with a poisoned comb.

| |

(c)   Beautiful Snow White lives in a cottage in the forest.

| |

(d)   The young prince wants to take the glass coffin to his palace.

| |

(e)   Snow White grows up with her father and wicked stepmother.

| |

5. Why do you think Snow White was put in a glass coffin on a mountain top?

_____

_____

_____

_____

_____

Snow White

1. Follow directions to dress and color the dwarfs.

| 1st | | 3rd | | | 6th | |

(a) Finish the number order of the dwarfs.
(b) Color the jacket of the 1st, 3rd and 6th dwarf red.
(c) Give four of the dwarfs green boots.
(d) Draw stripes on the 5th dwarf's shirt and spots on the 3rd.
(e) Give two dwarfs yellow scarves.
(f) Draw a hat on the 2nd and 7th dwarf.

2. Choose a character from the story to finish the report.

Name _____

Lives with _____

at _____ .

Is | kind | mean, | beautiful | ugly,
rich | poor, | happy | sad.

Likes to _____

_____

3. Make these words more than one. For example "one *wife*," "two *wives*."

(a) half _____ (b) elf _____

(c) shelf_____ (d) wolf _____

Classical Literature

> *Midas was both a king in Greek myths and a historical king of Phrygia (now Turkey) who lived around 700 B.C. The story of the "Golden Touch" may have arisen because the ancient Greeks believed that Phrygia was a land of enormous wealth. Nowadays, someone described as having the "Midas touch" has the ability to make money.*

King Midas

Midas is a Greek king who lived hundreds of years ago. He is very rich and loves his only daughter, whose mother is dead. One day, Midas is kind and helpful to the servant of a god. This god then grants Midas any wish he might want. Midas wants to be very, very rich. He says he wants anything he touches to turn into gold. Then the greedy king touches everything around him. Roses, bread and grapes change into gold.

However, he accidentally touches his daughter. When she turns into a gold statue he is very sad. Soon, the god takes pity on Midas. He tells the starving king to bathe in the waters of a faraway river. Will the king ever hold his daughter in his arms again?

Read one of these junior fiction books:

King Midas and the Golden Touch – a version by E. Metaxas

Greek Myths – J. Morley

King Midas

1. Why was Midas given a wish?

_____

_____

2. Write key words to best describe the king before and after his wish.

Before	After

3. List three things the king turned to gold.

(a) _____ (b) _____ (c) _____

4.   True or false?

(a)   The king lived in Greece hundreds of years ago. | true | false |

(b)   The king meant to turn his daughter to gold. | true | false |

(c)   Midas had many daughters. | true | false |

(d)   The god took pity on the starving Midas. | true | false |

5. What would you wish for if you were King Midas?

_____

_____

_____

6. How do you think the story will end?
Color the happy/sad meter to rate your ending.

_____

_____

Classical Literature   World Teachers Press®

King Midas

1. Write sentences about this part of the story.

_____

_____

_____

_____

_____

_____

_____

2. Write these words in alphabetical order.

(a) touch, statue, pity, roses, king

_____

(b) gold, god, greedy, garden, grant

_____

3. Unjumble the words along the path to find what the king turned to gold.

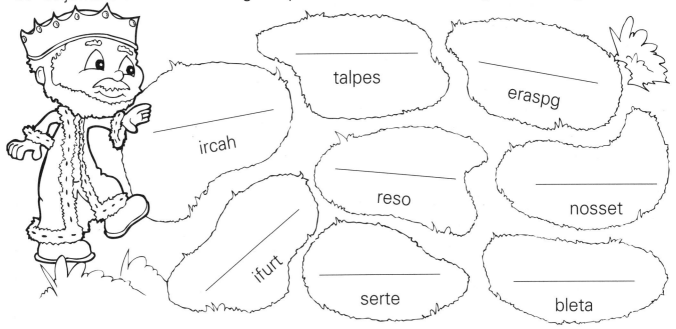

talpes

eraspg

ircah

reso

nosset

ifurt

serte

bleta

Dick Whittington was a real person who lived in the 14th century. He married Alice Fitzwarren, the daughter of a rich merchant. He was mayor of London three times until he died, a very rich man, in 1423. No one knows whether Dick really had a cat, but the legend, though different from his real life, has been popular for hundreds of years.

Dick Whittington

Dick Whittington is the youngest of three brothers. One day, his father dies and leaves his family with no money. Dick hears that the streets of London are paved with gold. He decides to go there to seek his fortune and takes his pet cat with him. Many people live in London. Making money would be difficult so he starts to return home. Then he hears church bells which tell him he will become Mayor of London. He returns to the big city.

In later years, he stays with a rich merchant called Mr. Fitzwarren. This merchant is sending a ship to Africa. His ship's captain will sell goods to an African king. The merchant asks Dick if he has anything to sell. Dick sends the only thing he has—his cat! The cat makes him very rich and he marries Alice, the merchant's daughter. I wonder how the cat made him so rich?

Read one of these junior fiction books:

Dick Whittington – a version by R. Brooke

Dick Whittington and His Cat – a version by M. Brown

Dick Whittington

1. Why did Dick Whittington first go to London?

   _____

   _____

2. Dick had | one | two | three | brothers.

3. What did the church bells tell him?

   _____

   _____

4. Who traveled with Dick? _____

5. Fill in the missing words

   Mr. _____[1] was a _____[2]

   merchant sending a ship to _____[3].

   The ship's _____[4] will sell

   goods to an African _____[5].

6. Why did Dick sell his cat?

   _____

   _____

7. How do you think the cat could make Dick wealthy?

   _____

   _____

   _____

   _____

   _____

Dick Whittington

1. Circle the words that mean the same.

(a)	rich	well	wealthy	poor
(b)	merchant	dealer	carpenter	trader
(c)	big	huge	minute	large
(d)	seek	worn	search	try

2. Number these pictures in order.

Dick marries Alice, the merchant's daughter.

The church bells tell him he will be Mayor.

Dick sells his cat to the merchant.

Dick and his cat search London for riches.

3. Dick Whittington had a special pet cat.
Complete the profile on your pet (or one you would like to have).

Name _____

Age _____

Description _____

_____

Food _____

Special tricks _____

_____

_____

_____

"The Story of Babar" by Jean De Brunhoff was translated from French into English. It was the first of a series of picture storybooks about a young elephant. It was first published in Great Britain in 1934.

The Story of Babar

Babar is a baby elephant who lives in the jungle with his friends. His loving mother takes care of Babar at all times. One dreadful day, an evil man hiding behind a bush kills Babar's mother with his rifle. The young elephant is so frightened he just runs and runs. Soon he comes to a large town. There he meets a rich old lady who buys him clothes to wear. He lives in her house and is taught lessons by a teacher.

After a while, Babar misses the jungle and his animal friends so he returns home. He finds out that the King of the Elephants has just died after eating a poisonous mushroom. All the elephants decide they now need a new leader. Babar has learned a lot while living with the people in the town. I wonder if the herd will ask Babar to be their new king?

Read one of these junior fiction books or view one of these movies:

The Story of Babar – J. De Brunhoff

The Story of Babar the Little Elephant – J. De Brunhoff

Babar: King of the Elephants – video

Babar - The Movie – video

The Story of Babar

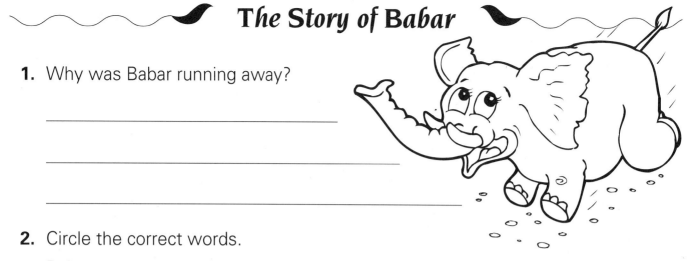

1. Why was Babar running away?

_____

_____

_____

2. Circle the correct words.

Babar came to a large (jungle, town) where he meets a (poor, rich)

(old, young) lady who buys him (food, clothes).

3. How did the King of Elephants die?

_____

_____

4. Do you think Babar would make a good king? Explain why.

_____

_____

_____

5. Show with red dots where Babar went in the story.

6. Write two words that best describe Babar.

_____

_____

The Story of Babar

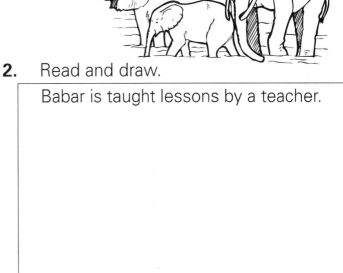

1. Animals that live in groups often have group names. For example, elephants – herd. Match these animal groups.

   (a) whales •   • herd

   (b) pups •   • gaggle

   (c) sheep •   • pod

   (d) geese •   • school

   (e) cows •   • litter

   (f) fish •   • flock

2. Read and draw.

   Babar is taught lessons by a teacher.

3. Find words from the story with these sounds.

er	ing

4. Use the clues to find the mystery word.

   _____

   1. The hunter hid behind a _____.

   2. Babar is one of these.

   3. Babar was just a _____ when he first left the jungle.

   4. Babar _____ a lot while living in town.

   5. A group of elephants.

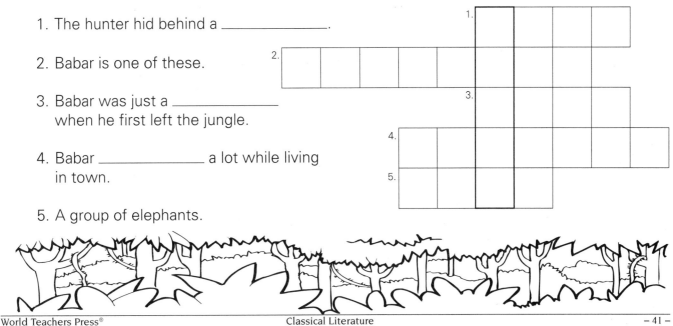

This story was first made popular in 1697 by a French poet, Charles Perrault. He retold many ancient fairy tales such as "Little Red Riding Hood" and "Puss in Boots" in order to entertain his children. The origin of the story was Madame De Beaumont's 18th century tale "Belle et la Bête."

Beauty and the Beast

Beauty is the daughter of a rich merchant. She is not like her two older sisters for she is kind and gentle. One day, the merchant loses his cargo ships in a storm. They are now very poor and have to move to a smaller house. During his travels, the father becomes lost and finds a wonderful palace. In the palace garden the merchant picks a beautiful rose for Beauty.

The beast who owns the palace is very angry and says the merchant is stealing the flower. The merchant is told he can only leave if one of his daughters returns to the palace. Beauty agrees to go and becomes the beast's friend. They listen to music and read books. They talk about dragons, magic and kings and queens. Each night the ugly creature asks Beauty to marry him. He is so kind-hearted she finally says yes and something magical happens. I wonder what it is?

Read one of these junior fiction books:

Beauty and the Beast – a version by D. Hautzig

The Candlewick Book of Fairy Tales – S. Hayes

Beauty and the Beast

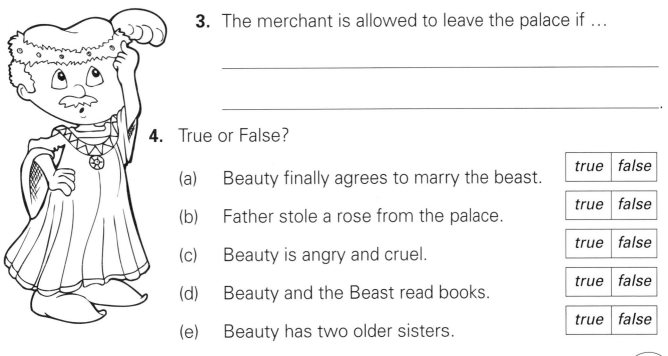

1. Fill in the missing words.

_____ is the daughter of a

_____ merchant.

She has _____ older sisters.

She is _____ and gentle.

2. Why did the merchant move his family?

_____

3. The merchant is allowed to leave the palace if …

_____

_____.

4. True or False?

		true	false
(a)	Beauty finally agrees to marry the beast.	true	false
(b)	Father stole a rose from the palace.	true	false
(c)	Beauty is angry and cruel.	true	false
(d)	Beauty and the Beast read books.	true	false
(e)	Beauty has two older sisters.	true	false

5. List three things Beauty and the Beast share together.

_____

_____

_____

6. How do you think the story ends? Give it a rating on the happy/sad meter.

_____

_____

Beauty and the Beast

1. Draw Beauty and the Beast. Write sentences to describe each character

Beauty	Beast

_____   _____

_____   _____

_____   _____

_____   _____

2. Find opposites in the story.

   (a) cruel _____

   (b) beautiful _____

   (c) poor _____

   (d) found _____

   (e) larger _____

   (f) night _____

   (g) kings _____

3. Find rhyming words from the story.

   (a) least _____

   (b) power _____

   (c) tricks _____

   (d) looks _____

   (e) nose _____

   (f) feature _____

   (g) mind _____

Hans Christian Andersen was a Danish writer who was born nearly 200 years ago. Though he was a poor speller he wrote more than 150 stories, some sad and some happy. He came from a poor home and was always making up stories and plays when he was a young boy. One famous story is "The Little Mermaid." There is a small statue of a mermaid in Copenhagen Harbor to remember that tale.

Thumbelina

A woman who longs to have a child goes to see a witch. She is given a grain of barley to plant. Soon a pretty red and yellow flower-like tulip grows in the plant pot. The woman kisses the flower and it opens. Inside the petals is a beautiful girl, half the size of a thumb. This tiny girl is stolen by an ugly, slimy toad, looking for a wife for its son. The toad keeps her on a large water lily leaf in a stream. Some fish decide to help her so they set the leaf free. It floats down the stream past many towns.

Thumbelina has many adventures with insects, animals and birds. As winter is coming she flies off to warmer lands on the back of a swallow. There, she meets the tiny, handsome king of the flower fairies. Will there be a happy ending for Thumbelina?

Read one of these junior fiction books:

Thumbelina – H.C. Andersen

Thumbelina – a version by A. Koenig

Thumbelina – a version by A. Earlich

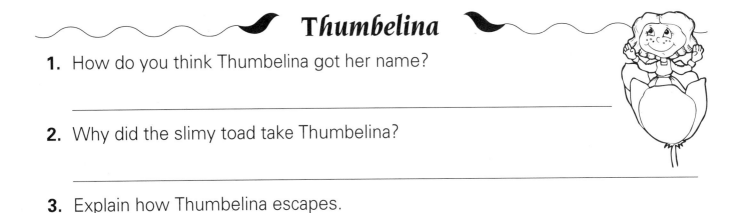

Thumbelina

1. How do you think Thumbelina got her name?

   _____

2. Why did the slimy toad take Thumbelina?

   _____

3. Explain how Thumbelina escapes.

   _____

   _____

4. Write a part of the story that you think fits these headings.

sad	adventurous	happy

5. Find words to describe these phrases from the story.

   (a) _____ slimy toad   (c) _____ water lily

   (b) _____ Thumbelina   (d) _____ flower

6. Show with red dots on the story map where Thumbelina traveled in the story.

Rumplestiltskin 6 – 8

Page 7
1. that his daughter could spin gold from straw
2. in a palace
3. (a) no   (b) yes   (c) yes
   (d) yes   (e) yes
4. Rumplestiltskin
5. (a) rich   (b) little   (c) gifts
   (d) tale   (e) strange
6. Teacher check
7. Teacher check

Page 8
1. (a) hat   (b) shirt   (c) boots
   (d) pants   (e) belt
2. (a) guess   (b) spin   (c) locks
   (d) straw
3. (a) he runs the mill that grinds the flour
   (b) (i) make things from wood
   (ii) make clothes
   (iii) hunted
   (iv) makes/repairs things of iron
   (v) makes/repairs shoes

The Tale of Peter Rabbit 9 – 11

Page 10
1. Flopsy, Mopsy, Cottontail, Peter
2. because father was caught there and made into rabbit pie
3. (a) burrow
   (b) five
   (c) white
4. (a) vegetables   (b) in the tool shed
5. (a) white   (b) huge   (c) young
   (d) under   (e) can't   (f) out
6. Teacher check

Page 11
1. burrow
   (a) bear – den
   (b) pig – sty
   (c) bee – hive
   (d) spider – web
   (e) horse – stable
   (f) snail – shell
2. hutch, Teacher check
3. Teacher check
4. (a) v   (b) v   (c) f
   (d) f   (e) v   (f) f
5. Teacher check

The Cat in the Hat 12 – 14

Page 13
1. they were all alone and it was raining
2. Teacher check
3. a strange cat
4. Teacher check
5. (a) yes   (b) no
   (c) no   (d) no
6. (a) It was a cold, wet day.
   (b) The strange cat wore a funny hat.
7. Teacher check

Page 14
1. Teacher check
2. (a) rainbow   (b) earring   (c) football
3. Teacher check
4. books, bowl, cake, goldfish

The Hare and the Tortoise 15 – 17

Page 16
1. to show how fast he was
2. the tortoise
3. because a tortoise moves very slowly
4. he was very confident of winning
5. (a) to speak with too much pride
   (b) to have a short sleep
   (c) challenges
   (d) to go on or continue in a slow manner
6.

fast	kind	playful
sharing	confident	
boastful	shy	daring

slow	keen	speedy
excitable		steady
plodder	silly	winner

7. Teacher check

Page 17
1.

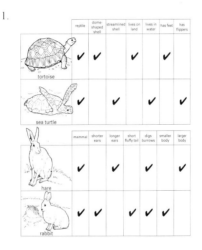

	reptile	dome-shaped shell	streamlined shell	lives on land	lives in water	has feet	has flippers
tortoise	✔	✔		✔		✔	
sea turtle	✔		✔		✔		✔

	mammal	shorter ears	longer ears	short fluffy tail	digs burrows	smaller body	larger body
hare	✔		✔		✔		✔
rabbit	✔	✔		✔	✔	✔	

Cinderella 18 – 20

Page 19
1. a fairy godmother helped her
2. he invites her to another ball, he dances with her all night
3. (a) 5   (b) 2   (c) 6
   (d) 3   (e) 4   (f) 1
4. (a) midnight   (d) leaves
   (b) daughters   (e) tearful
   (c) beautiful   (f) appears
5.

Page 20
1. Teacher check
2. (a) boot   (d) clog
   (b) sandal   (e) sneaker
   (c) thong   (f) moccasin
3. (a) golden   (e) glass
   (b) bossy/vain   (f) cruel
   (c) splendid   (g) beautiful/kind/gentle
   (d) ragged   (h) loyal

Hansel and Gretel 21 – 23

Page 22
1. to lose them in the forest
2. Teacher check
3. It was made of gingerbread, cake and barley sugar.
4. a witch
5. (a) true   (b) false   (c) true
   (d) true   (e) true
6. Teacher check

Page 23
1. (a) pancake   (b) eggplant
   (c) basketball
2. woodcutter, gingerbread, breadcrumbs
3. (a) wicked   (d) small
   (b) children   (e) evil
   (c) strange
4. (a) house   (d) cake
   (b) deep   (e) back
   (c) witch
5. Teacher check.

Jack and the Beanstalk 24 – 26

Page 25
1. **Jack** is an **only** son who lives with his **mother**. They are very **poor**.
   He takes a **cow** to sell at the **market** but swaps the cow for some **magic beans**.
2. because they needed money
3. a castle of a rich giant
4. Teacher check
5. ogre
6. she felt sorry for him/giant eats boys on toast
7. oven
8. Teacher check

Page 26

1. magic –
2. 2, 4, 1, 3
3.

mean	pleasant	ogre
tiny	grumpy	sad
huge	happy	rich
kind	silly	poor
adventurous	frightened	
cruel	happy	climber

4. cow, eating, market, lays, beanstalk, boys

Tiddalik 27 – 29

Page 28
1. because he was thirsty
2. Teacher check
3. (a) emus dance
   (b) animals play leapfrog
   (c) kookaburra laughs at his own funny stories
4. Teacher check
5. (a) a waterhole which used to be part of a river
   (b) Teacher check
6. Teacher check

Page 29
1. (a) laugh
   (b) unhappy
   (c) inside
   (d) hot
   (e) down
   (f) noisy
2. Teacher check
3. emu, frog, kangaroo, kookaburra
4. thirsty –

```
¹W A T E R
²U N H A P P Y
    ³D I E
    ⁴F R O G
      ⁵S U M M E R
  ⁶R E S T
⁷F U N N Y
```

Snow White 30 – 32

Page 31
1. in the forest with the seven dwarfs
2. (a) yes   (b) no
   (c) no   (d) yes
3. comb, apple
4. (a) 4   (b) 3   (c) 2
   (d) 5   (e) 1
5. Teacher check

Page 32
1. 2nd, 4th, 5th, 7th Teacher check
2. Teacher check
3. (a) halves
   (b) elves
   (c) shelves
   (d) wolves

King Midas 33 – 35

Page 34
1. he was kind to the servant of the god
2. Teacher check
3. (a) everything around him
   (b) roses
   (c) his daughter
4. (a) true   (c) false
   (b) false   (d) true
5. Teacher check
6. Teacher check

Page 35
1. Teacher check
2. (a) king, pity, roses, statue, touch
   (b) garden, god, gold, grant, greedy
3. chair, plates, grapes, fruit, rose, stones, trees, table

Dick Whittington 36 – 38

Page 37
1. he heard that the streets were paved with gold
2. two
3. he was to become Mayor
4. his cat
5. Mr. **Fitzwarren** was a **rich** merchant sending a ship to **Africa**.
   The ship's **captain** will sell goods to an African **king**.
6. to get some money
7. Teacher check

Page 38
1. (a) rich, wealthy
   (b) merchant, dealer, trader
   (c) big, huge, large
   (d) seek, search
2. 4, 2, 3, 1
3. Teacher check

The Story of Babar 39 – 41

Page 40
1. his mother was shot
2. town, rich, old, clothes
3. He ate a poisonous mushroom
4. Teacher check
5. Teacher check
6. Teacher check

Page 41
1. (a) whales – pod
   (b) pups – litter
   (c) sheep – flock
   (d) geese – gaggle
   (e) cows – herd
   (f) fish – school
2. Teacher check
3. herd, wonder, mother, her, teacher living, king, hiding, eating
4. Babar –

```
        ¹B U S H
²E L E P H A N T
        ³B A B Y
    ⁴L E A R N E D
    ⁵H E R D
```

Beauty and the Beast 42 – 44

Page 43
1. **Beauty** is the daughter of a **rich** merchant.
   She has **two** older sisters.
   She is **kind** and gentle.
2. one of his cargo ships is lost in a storm and he becomes poor
3. one of his daughters comes to the palace
4. (a) true
   (b) true
   (c) false
   (d) true
   (e) true
5. Teacher check
6. Teacher check

Page 44
1. Teacher check
2. (a) kind
   (b) ugly
   (c) rich
   (d) lost
   (e) smaller
   (f) day
   (g) queens
3. (a) beast
   (b) flower
   (c) picks
   (d) books
   (e) rose
   (f) creature
   (g) kind

Thumbelina 45 – 46

Page 46
1. because she was half the size of a thumb
2. he was looking for a wife for his son
3. the fish let the lily leaf loose
4. Teacher check
5. (a) ugly
   (b) happy
   (c) large
   (d) pretty
6. Teacher check